D1124340

BEAUTY HACKS

HAIR

HACKS
YOUR TRESSES TROUBLES SOLVED!

MARY BOONE

CAPSTONE PRESS
a capstone imprint

Savvy Books are published by Capstone Press,
1710 Roe Crest Drive, North Mankato,
Minnesota 56003

www.mycapstone.com

**Library of Congress Cataloging-in-
Publication Data**
Library of Congress Cataloging-in-Publication
data is available on the Library of Congress
website.

ISBN 978-1-5157-6829-6 (library binding)
ISBN 978-1-5157-6833-3 (eBook PDF)

Editorial Credits
Mandy Robbins, editor; Aruna Rangarajan,
designer; Kelli Lageson and Morgan
Walters, media researchers; Kathy McColley,
production specialist

Photo Credits
All photos by Capstone Studio:
Karon Dubke, except:
Capstone Press: Aruna Rangarajan, 30 (top
right); Shutterstock: Africa Studio, 27, 29
(bottom), Aila Images, cover, Aksenova
Natalya, cover (back cover bottom left), 13,
Aleksandr Bryliaev, 9 (bottom right), Aleksei
Golovanov, cover (back cover top right),
30 (top left), Alena Ozerova, 16, Anastasiia
Kazakova, 4, 28, 44 (top), Ariwasabi, 12,
athurstock, 23 (top right), bigacis, 41 (middle),
bonchan, 43 (top right and bottom left), Dean
Drobot, 24, design56, 43 (bottom right), 44
(bottom left), Djomas, 10, Elena11, 21 (bottom),
gpointstudio, 14, HTeam, 39 (top), Kaponia
Aliaksei, 22 (top), Kitch Bain, 18, Kseniia
Perminova, 37, mimagephotography, 31, natu,
38, Nikkolia, 2, 32, 48, popcorner, 34 (bottom),
42 (bottom left), Robert Przybysz, 6, Studio
KIWI, 23 (back), Superlime, 20, Svitlana
Sokolova, 41 (bottom), timquo, 42 (top), Tom
Tomczyk, 41 (top), tryam, 39 (bottom), Venus
Angel, cover (back cover bottom right), 23 (top
left), Viktoriya Legkobyt, 45 (bottom)

Design elements: Shutterstock

Printed and bound in the USA.
082017 010695R

TABLE OF CONTENTS

HAIR HACKS 101

Do you wish for
SUPER-SHINY TRESSES or
EFFORTLESS WAVES?

It's easy to make all your hair-related dreams come true, no magic involved. Some simple hacks can upgrade your hairstyle.

The most important tip anyone needs when it comes to hair hacks is to keep your hair healthy. What you eat really does make a difference. Take charge and revive your locks, starting with your diet. A balanced diet with the right mix of protein, iron, and other nutrients can improve the health of your scalp and hair. Once hair health is in check, get your styling products and tools handy. You will need the following items:

SUPPLIES NEEDED

Hair Products

* barrettes or hair clips
* bobby pins
* brush
* comb
* conditioner
* curling iron or wand
* dry shampoo
* elastic bands
* foam rollers
* heat-protectant spray
* hair dryer with diffuser attachment
* hair gel or mousse
* hair spray
* heat-resistant glove
* shampoo
* spray bottle
* straightener
* stretchy headband

Pantry Items

* avocado
* banana
* brown sugar
* chopsticks
* coconut oil
* cornstarch
* honey
* lemon juice
* mayonnaise
* olive oil
* powdered drink mix
* sea salt
* plain yogurt

Other Helpful Items

* baby powder
* cleaning cloth/rag
* dryer sheets
* hydrocortisone cream
* microfiber towel or cotton T-shirt
* old toothbrush or makeup brush
* rubbing alcohol
* ruler
* satin or silk pillowcase
* scissors

A 2000 study conducted by Yale University found that "bad hair days" affect an individual's self-esteem, increase self-doubt, and intensify self-criticism.

CHAPTER 1

GET YOUR TOOLS IN ORDER

You wouldn't try to bake a cake without a bowl or a spoon. Similarly, hair care requires certain tools and a basic understanding of how to use and maintain them.

BOBBY PINS 101

You might be using bobby pins **backward.** Whether you're using them to hold a bun in place or keep bangs out of your eyes, slip them into your hair with the wavy side down, toward your scalp. Those grooves are designed to grip hair and lock it in place against your head.

→ *This side on scalp*

CAN'T STAND THE HEAT?

Tired of battling heat and burns while using styling irons? You can protect yourself by wearing a **heat-resistant glove.** These lightweight, reusable gloves are designed to fit either your right or left hand. You can find them for sale at beauty supply stores.

CLEAN YOUR BRUSHES AND COMBS

Dirt and hair products can build up on your brushes and combs. That's not what you want to run through your freshly washed hair.

Step 1 Clean your brushes by getting old hair out of the bristles. Use scissors to cut it away if necessary.

Step 2 Next, fill the sink with warm water and swirl the head of the brush in it.

Step 3 Squirt a few drops of shampoo onto an old toothbrush, and use it to scrub the bristles and base of the hairbrush.

Step 4 Rinse thoroughly, and place the brush, bristle side down, on a towel to dry overnight.

Plastic combs are even easier to clean. Just take the comb with you into the shower, and rub it with shampoo under warm water. Rinse well.

DE-GUNK CURLING IRONS AND STRAIGHTENERS

Your curling iron or straightener can get sticky with the buildup of baked-on products. Clean your tools using one of these methods:

1. Soak a clean cloth with rubbing alcohol, and wipe the straightener or curling iron. Make sure to do this while the iron or straightener is cool. Let the alcohol sit on the surface for several minutes. Scrub stubborn spots with an old toothbrush. Use a clean, damp cloth to wipe the appliance down.

2. Attack stubborn goo with a paste made of equal parts baking soda and water. Spread the paste onto the straightener or curling iron. Allow it to sit for 10 minutes before scrubbing with a damp cloth. Rinse the cloth, and wipe the straightener, cleaning any leftover paste.

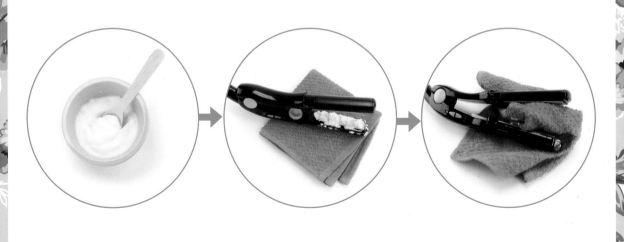

CORRAL THE CLUTTER

Tangled cords, sprays, gels, brushes, and bobby pins can quickly add up to countertop clutter. Don't let hair care tools and supplies defeat you — GET ORGANIZED:

Use a large, clean flowerpot on the counter to hold your hair dryer, curling iron, and brushes. Add some decorations for a touch of flair!

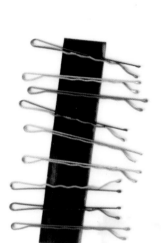

Put a **magnetic strip** inside a cabinet door or drawer to collect bobby pins.

Repurpose a **silverware basket** as an on-the-counter organizer. Use different sections to hold your styling products, hair clips, and ties.

Don't waste space on items you're not using. Toss or give away products you don't love as much as you thought you would. Get rid of tools you haven't used in the past two years.

Choose the Right ▷▷▷▷▷
HAIR DRYER

Hair dryers can range in price from $15 to more than $300. How can you know which one is right for you? Understanding the following terms is the first step toward finding the perfect product.

WATTAGE

Wattage measures how hard a hair dryer blows. A high-wattage motor is more powerful and will reduce styling time. Look for a dryer with a wattage of at least 1800 for the quickest results.

IONIC

If you have thick, frizzy hair, an ionic dryer is a good choice. Water ions are positively charged. Ionic dryers shoot negative ions, which makes them more effective at breaking up water droplets and creating smoother tresses.

CERAMIC

Ceramic porcelain is often used to coat or replace a hair dryer's internal parts. This keeps temperatures consistent. These materials also give off negative ions for quick drying and less frizz.

TOURMALINE

Tourmaline hair dryers are good for hair that tends to get frizzy. Tourmaline is a stone that is used in some hair dryers. It produces a high concentration of ions and infrared heat. Tourmaline dryers dry your hair quickly and more smoothly than other hair dryers.

TITANIUM

Titanium is used to evenly distribute heat and keep temperatures steady. Because it can get very hot, you should avoid a titanium dryer if your hair is fine or easily damaged.

SUPERSONIC

These high-speed hair dryers are some of the most expensive. They blow at much higher speeds than other hair dryers, while keeping the temperature consistent and cool enough not to damage hair.

Washing your hair seems simple enough — just use water, shampoo, and conditioner. But there are tricks and tips that can make your hair-washing routine more effective and give your hair more shine and volume.

CHAPTER 2

CLEANING UP

▶ CHECK THE TEMP

A warm shower not only feels terrific, it also opens hair cuticles so shampoo and conditioner can do their jobs. However, at the end of your shower, when your hair is clean, lower the water temperature. A cool rinse will close hair cuticles and seal in moisture, giving your hair extra shine.

▶ REVERSE YOUR ROUTINE

If you're like most people, you use shampoo first and then conditioner. But hair pros actually suggest that using conditioner first can nourish your hair without weighing it down. Just use your normal conditioner, rinse, and then shampoo. This little change primes the hair, allowing shampoo to distribute more evenly. You'll probably notice that your hair is shinier after reversing your routine.

▶ DON'T OVERDO THE POO

The hair closest to your scalp is the oiliest, while the ends are generally drier and more fragile. Instead of shampooing and conditioning all over, concentrate shampoo toward the roots. When you apply conditioner, focus on the mid-shaft to the ends, where more moisture is needed.

▶ START AT THE TOP

When you blow dry, work down from the roots to the ends. Be sure to keep the blow dryer moving constantly. You want to avoid using too much heat in a single spot. This technique allows cuticles to close properly. When you do that, you minimize frizz and bring out your hair's shine.

Pick the Right PRODUCTS

Some shampoos are developed to target specific issues. Use these guidelines to select the ideal shampoo for you.

FINE, LIMP HAIR

Fine strands will look bulkier if you use a volumizing shampoo. These products include ingredients that increase the width of the hair shaft.

DRY HAIR AND SCALP

If your scalp is dry but not itchy, look for products that promote moisture, hydration, or smoothing. If your scalp is very dry and itchy, consider shampoos that include menthol or tea tree oil.

FRIZZY HAIR

Hydration is your friend when you're taming frizz. Look for products with extra moisturizers and smoothing agents to seal hair cuticles.

OILY HAIR AND SCALP

Avoid hydrating shampoos. They will add moisture to your already oily scalp. Products labeled as volumizing, strengthening, or clarifying will more effectively remove excess oil.

No Time to Wash? Try These Hacks

Let's face it — sometimes you just don't have time to wash your hair. To make your hair look great on days when it's a little dirty, try one of these quick tips:

1. DRY SHAMPOO

Dry shampoo cleans hair without water. It absorbs oil and makes your hair look fresh again. Apply dry shampoo — powder or spray — at your roots. Blend with your fingers, and brush out the excess. You can even find dry shampoo to match your hair color so it blends in easier.

2. SWITCH YOUR PART

Greasy hair is often limp. Add volume by parting your hair on the opposite side.

3. BRAID IT

Braids help mask oily strands. And they actually hold better when your hair is not freshly washed.

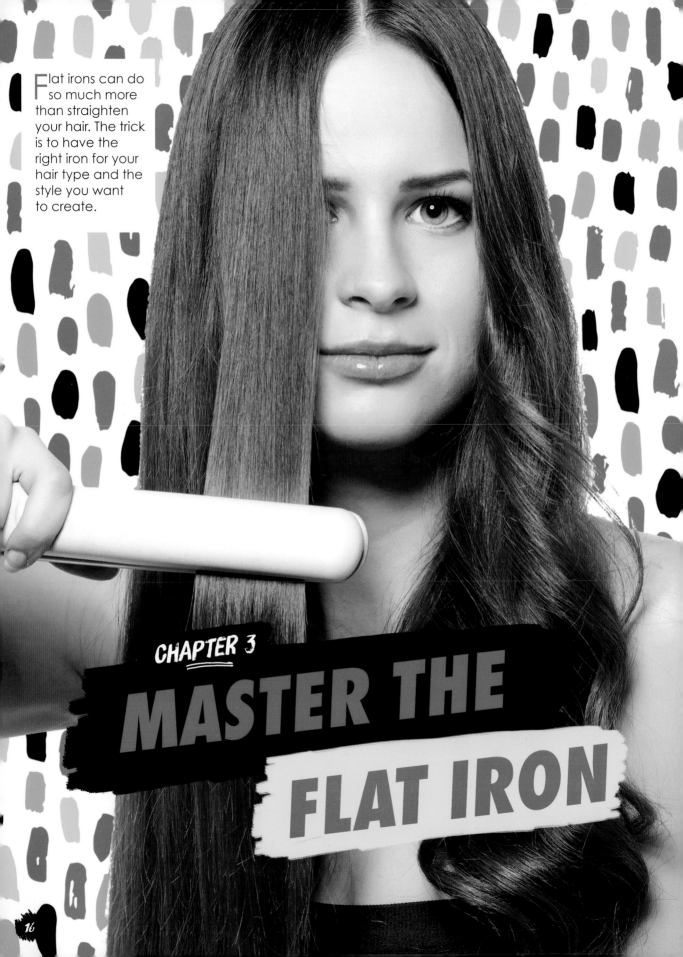

Flat irons can do so much more than straighten your hair. The trick is to have the right iron for your hair type and the style you want to create.

CHAPTER 3

MASTER THE FLAT IRON

MAKE WAVES

Casual waves can be yours without a lot of work. Simply braid your hair into pigtails. Spritz your braids with heat protectant before running a flat iron over them a few times. Unbraid your hair to reveal a headful of easy waves.

USE A STRAIGHTENER TO CREATE CURLS

Flat irons can make your hair sleek and smooth, but they can also create curls. First, spray dry hair with a heat protectant. These serums and sprays protect hair from heat damage caused by styling tools. Clip up the top layer of your hair, and begin curling the bottom layer, one small section at a time. Using a 1- to 2-inch flat iron, clamp a section of hair into the iron 2 inches from the roots. Twist hair around the flat iron and pull to the ends. Work your way through both the bottom and top layers of hair. Apply hair spray to set.

The Right Tools Used
THE RIGHT WAY

When choosing a flat iron, you must consider both your hair type and length. Follow these guidelines to select the iron best suited to your mane.

THIN OR FINE HAIR

Your hair can be styled with nearly any flat iron. Look for one that allows you to adjust the temperature. **Start with a low temperature — around 180 degrees Fahrenheit —** and turn up the heat if you're not getting the results you're after. Higher temperatures help to hold your look, but they can also damage your hair. This can be especially hard on thin or fine hair. Look for an iron with ceramic or tourmaline plates to protect your hair from heat damage.

MEDIUM-THICK OR WAVY HAIR

If your hair is shoulder length or longer, **look for an iron that is 1¼ to 2 inches wide.** This is the right size to give long hair loose waves. Shorter hair? Buy an iron with plates **½ to 1¼ inches wide.** Anything wider than that is too big to work on short hair.

THICK, COARSE, CURLY HAIR

Longer hair requires wider plates — **1- to 2- inch plates** work best. If hair is shoulder length or shorter, buy an iron with plates **1 to 1½ inches** wide. Your hair needs higher heat, so make sure temperature settings are adjustable. Look for irons with **ceramic, titanium, or tourmaline** plates.

AVOID
These Flat Iron Don'ts

1.

Don't straighten damp hair. Use a flat iron on wet hair and you'll end up with steam. That's a sure sign your hair follicles are burning.

2.

Don't use too much heat. Adjust the heat according to your hair type recommendation. Never heat a flat iron above 450 degrees Fahrenheit. Not even the strongest hair can take temps that hot.

A flat iron can help you achieve styling greatness, but you have to use it properly. Follow these rules to keep your hair healthy.

3.

Don't skip the thermal protectant. Heat protectant forms a protective barrier over the hair's cuticle. This ensures that your hair keeps its shine, despite using heating tools.

4.

Don't try to do too much at once. If you try to straighten a very large section of hair, only the outer portions will get heated. The inside will stay untouched. Choose small sections to be on the safe side.

5.

Don't use a flat iron every single day. Smooth, straight hair can be beautiful, but so can wavy, natural hair. Give your hair some time off, and let it dry naturally.

CHAPTER 4

HOT CURLS FOR
HIGH STYLE

When you want glamorous curls, the quickest way to get them is with heat. Curling irons and wands curl your hair quickly, but there are many things to consider to get the look you want.

Curling irons are not one-size-fits-all.

But don't fret. The right curling iron and some basic know-how can help you get the beautiful curls you want.

THE RIGHT BARREL FOR YOUR CURL

Which size curling iron or wand should you buy? That depends on your hair type and length, as well as the look you're after. Use these guidelines to make the right choice.

¾-INCH BARREL ▶ This size barrel is great for recreating **vintage looks.** It works well for touching up naturally curly hair

1- TO 1¼-INCH BARREL ▶ This is the most popular size for anyone with **shoulder-length hair.** Resulting styles can be polished and sleek or loose and beachy, depending how you use it.

1½-INCH BARREL ▶ This size can be used to create **voluminous curls.** It's handy for giving long hair a little lift at the roots.

1¾- TO 2-INCH BARREL ▶ This larger size is best for those with **long hair.** An iron this large is best for creating a rounded bend at the ends of your hair.

BAN THE BURN

No matter how careful you are, using a curling iron or straightener means you might burn yourself. Take these steps to minimize the pain and the scar.

➕ Wrap ice in a thin cloth and hold it against the burn to lower the skin's temperature.

➕ Apply a 1-percent hydrocortisone cream to the burned area. At night, use a gentle cleanser (nothing with alcohol in it) to wash the burned skin. Then apply a moisturizing ointment. See a doctor if the burn starts to blister or develops pus.

➕ Get creative with your hairstyle to camouflage your wound. Side-swept bangs can cover a forehead burn. Wear your hair down to cover a burn on your neck.

CUT CURLING TIME WITH A PONYTAIL

To curl hair quickly, put it in a high ponytail. Divide hair into two to four sections, depending on its thickness. Wrap one section of hair around the curling iron barrel and hold for a few seconds before releasing. Repeat with remaining sections. Take hair out of the ponytail and use your fingers to style.

UNWASHED HAIR STYLES BEST

There are times when having freshly washed hair is not ideal — like when you want to curl it. Squeaky-clean hair can slip out of curling irons and bobby pins. The natural oils in second-day hair make it easier to control and help it hold a style.

HORIZONTAL

HORIZONTAL OR VERTICAL?

You can change the look of your curls by simply changing the way you hold your curling iron. If you're going for a Hollywood-glam look with tighter, bouncier curls, hold the iron **horizontally.** For looser, wavier curls, hold the barrel of the iron **vertically.**

VERTICAL

TIP

If you curl your hair vertically, make sure the curls on both sides of your face either point toward or away from your face. You don't want one side curled toward you and the other away.

IRON or WAND?

Both tools create curls, but how easily you can use them and the style you're after will help you decide which is best for you.

A *classic curling iron* has a clip that holds hair in place while you're styling. It's perfect for creating polished curls with smooth ends.

A *curling wand* does not have a clip, so you need to wind your hair along the length of the wand and hold it in place until it's set. Most curling wands come with a heat-resistant glove to protect your hand from the heat of the wand. Curling wands can be used to create beachy waves with looser ends.

CHAPTER 5
CURL HAIR WITHOUT HEAT

Curling irons and flat irons create beautiful curls, but all that heat can damage your tresses. Luckily, there are many heat-free ways to add some curl to your life.

TRY SOFT ROLLERS

Bendy foam rollers allow you to curl your hair overnight. For best results, wash your hair and run some styling mousse through it. Wait until it is about 75 percent dry before beginning to put in the rollers. Divide hair into even sections — an inch of hair is a good place to start. Thick hair will require rolling smaller sections, while thin hair can be curled in larger chunks.

1. Place the roller at the end of the hair strands and roll upward.

2. When you get to the roots, bend the curler into a U shape to hold it tightly against your scalp.

3. Repeat until all hair is rolled. In the morning, unwind curlers and tousle your fabulous hair.

THE WAY TO WAVES ▶

If you can braid, you can get waves. Wash your hair in the evening, and braid it while it's damp. You can sleep in braids overnight and wake up with waves. Results will vary depending on the type of braid you choose, from French or fish tail to a basic three-strand braid.

◀ USE SIDE BUNS TO CREATE CURLS

Side buns can take your hair from flat to fab in less than 30 minutes. First mist hair with texturizing spray. Then part your hair into pigtails. Tightly twist and wind each pigtail into a bun and secure with a hair tie or bobby pins. When your hair is dry, unravel the buns and tousle your waves. Use hair spray to set.

USE A **HEADBAND** TO CREATE CURLS

Step 1 Start by brushing your hair and lightly misting it with water or styling spray. Put the headband on horizontally. It should rest around your forehead and the back of your head. Start with a 1-inch section of hair on one side and wrap it around the headband. Add a little more hair, as you would if you were French braiding, and wrap it around the headband again.

If you have a wide, stretchy headband, you can create soft curls overnight.

Step 2 Continue adding hair and wrapping it around the headband until you get to the back of your head.

Step 3 Repeat the process on the other side, again working front to back. Make sure all of your hair is tucked into the headband before you go to bed.

Step 4 In the morning, gently take out the headband. Be careful that you don't tangle your hair. Use your fingers to separate curls, and set your style with hair spray.

Proper Prep Helps Hair Hold Curl

Curling your hair takes time, so it's super frustrating if those curls start drooping before you're even out the door. Proper prep can give curls staying power.

GET RID OF DAMAGE.

Brittle hair and split ends won't hold curl. Make an appointment and ask your stylist to trim away as much damage as possible. A trim every six weeks will work wonders for your hair.

WORK WITH SECOND-DAY HAIR.

Second-day hair is easier to curl because its natural oils give it more texture than super-clean hair. If you're worried about an oily scalp, dust some dry shampoo into your roots.

USE THE RIGHT PRODUCTS.

Apply a good mousse or gel to give your hair body, as well as a heat-protecting product to safeguard your strands. When you're done styling, set curls with hair spray.

HANDS OFF.

Playing with your hair will flatten curls. Don't comb or use your fingers to style it too much or all your hard work will be for nothing.

Naturally curly hair can be drier and more prone to tangles than straight hair. Learn to care for your curls and adjust your maintenance routine to make all the difference.

CHAPTER 6

CURL CARE SECRETS

GET A DIFFUSER

Curly hair breaks and tangles more easily than straight hair. It needs to be handled with loving care. Air drying is best for curly hair, but you can blow it dry if you use a diffuser attachment. A diffuser spreads out the heat, which helps dry hair quickly without the heat damage of a regular hair dryer. Use heat protectant, and be sure to set your hair dryer on medium speed and temperature.

DON'T TERRY-IZE YOUR CURLS

The loops on terrycloth towels rough up hair cuticles and create frizz. Instead of a regular bath towel, try drying your hair with a microfiber towel or a cotton T-shirt. Most importantly, instead of rubbing your wet hair, gently squeeze the moisture from it.

BEAUTY SLEEP

Next time you lay your head down, make sure it's on a satin or silk pillowcase. Because hair glides more easily on silky fabrics than on standard cotton, this will reduce frizz and minimize static while maintaining hair moisture.

WIDE-TOOTHED COMBS RULE

Using the wrong detangling tool can damage or break your strands. For best results, try detangling or shaping curly hair with your fingers or a wide-toothed seamless comb. Look for a comb that doesn't have a seam along each tooth so hair can be combed without snagging.

DETANGLE IN THE SHOWER

Combing your hair after the shower will separate curls and cause frizz. Instead, apply conditioner and comb it through your hair while you're still in the shower. When you get out, remember to squeeze your hair dry. Don't rub it.

USE A CHOPSTICK TO ADD VOLUME

A smooth chopstick can be a curly-haired girl's best friend. Working with one section at a time, insert a chopstick into your hair and push it from mid-strand toward the roots. This technique will add subtle volume to your 'do. You can also use a chopstick to separate super-tight curls without creating frizz.

4 Things You Shouldn't do to Curly Hair

Because curly hair tends to be drier than other hair types, it needs to be treated gently and with lots of moisture. To keep it in tip-top shape, avoid:

1.

BRUSHES

Bristles fray the hair, disturb curl patterns, and create frizz. Instead of a brush, use your fingers, a wide-toothed pick, or a chopstick to detangle and style.

2.

TOO MUCH SHAMPOO

Shampooing too often will wash out the natural oils curls need. This can make curly hair brittle. Try to limit shampooing to just a few times per week.

3.

GOING WITHOUT PRODUCT

If you have curls, conditioner is your friend. You'll also want to invest in a good styling cream and anti-frizz lotion. Choose products that are made specifically for curly hair. Ingredients such as palm oil, coconut oil, and shea butter are your hair's friend.

4.

WET CUTS

When curls are wet, they loosen. When they're dry, they retract — some more tightly than others. Ask your stylist to cut your hair when it's dry so you'll know how every curl will fall.

Let's face it, there are days when you simply don't have a ton of time to spend on your hair. But that doesn't mean you don't want to look great. These tips and shortcuts can be a quick fix to high style.

CHAPTER 7

HIGH STYLE, LOW FUSS

NO-SCISSORS BANGS

With some artful styling, you can try bangs without fear of the shears.

Step 1 Create a high ponytail, then pull a chunk of hair out from the front of the pony and pull it over your forehead. Adjust the hair so that the "bangs" fall right where you want them.

Step 2 Use bobby pins to hold your fake bangs in place. Twist and wrap the rest of your ponytail into a bun; fasten with hairpins or bobby pins. If you want, add a pretty headband or hair clip.

NO-SHOW HAIR ELASTICS

Want to make your ponytail look fancy without a lot of fuss?

Step 1 Gather your hair into a ponytail and secure with an elastic band.

Step 2 Take a small section of hair from the underside of your ponytail and wrap it around the hair elastic. Secure the wrap with a bobby pin or two, hiding it in the base of the pony.

TRIPLE YOUR PONYTAIL STYLE

Up your style in an instant by using small elastic bands to secure your hair in three ponytails, one on top of the other.

1. Flip each tail and tuck it through the hair above it.

2. Pull the tails out through the bottom to create topsy tails.

3. Tuck the top two tail ends through the ponytails below.

BRING ON THE BEACHY WAVES

The tousled waves that go with spending a day at the beach are very chic. Sea salt spray lets you to recreate that look. You can buy sea salt spray or make your own by following these easy directions.

WHAT YOU NEED:

| empty spray bottle | 1 cup warm water | 2 teaspoons sea salt | 1 tablespoon coconut oil | 1 tablespoon hair gel | lavender or mint extract (optional) |

 + + + +

WHAT TO DO:

1 Pour 1 cup of warm water into a clean spray bottle.

2 Add 2 teaspoons of sea salt and shake until salt dissolves.

3 Add 1 tablespoon of hair gel and 1 tablespoon of coconut oil.

4 If desired, add a drop of lavender or mint extract for scent.

5 To style, mist and scrunch towel-dried hair. Shake the sea salt spray before each use.

DOUBLE-UP YOUR PONY

Thin hair can make for a wimpy ponytail. Make yours appear fuller by creating two separate ponytails.

Step 1 Gather the top half of your hair into a ponytail and secure with an elastic tie. Take the remainder of your hair and form a second ponytail, closer to the bottom of your head.

Step 2 Fluff your top pony, making sure your bottom ponytail is hidden. To add even more volume, curl the ends of your hair.

MAKE THE MESSY BUN YOUR FRIEND

Next time you wake up late with crazy hair, don't despair. If your hair is shoulder length or longer, a messy bun may be your best bet. Your bun's placement will affect its overall look. A high, messy bun can look more formal, while low buns are more casual.

Step 1 Gather your hair into a ponytail.

Step 2 Twist your hair to create a loose bun that resembles a cinnamon roll. Use a hair elastic and/or bobby pins to hold the bun in place.

35

A TWIST ON THE BASIC BUN

For an updo that's both simple and unique, consider a twisty bun.

Step 1 Create a back part and gather hair into two pigtails, each just an inch or two from the part.

Step 2 Loosely braid each pigtail and secure the ends with elastic ties.

Step 3 When the two braids are done, twist them together and tuck the ends into the bun itself. Secure with bobby pins as needed.

Is Short Hair RIGHT FOR YOU?

Pixies and cropped cuts can be super cute and low maintenance. But how do you know if short hair will flatter you? The experts at John Frieda, a company that makes shampoo and other hair care products, came up with something they call the **"2.25 rule."**

To take the test, grab a ruler and a pencil. Place the pencil under your chin horizontally. Measure from the pencil to the bottom of your earlobe. If the measurement is less than 2¼ inches, the pros say short hair will look great on you. If the distance is more than 2¼ inches, longer hair may be a more flattering look for you. Remember, these are just guidelines. It's your hair — **wear it however you want!**

2.25"

HOW TO DEAL WHEN GROWING OUT BANGS

If you've ever tried to grow out bangs, you know about the awkward stage. It's that period when your bangs are long enough to hang in your eyes but too short to tuck behind your ears. Try these tips to get through that tough time.

1.

DO THE TWIST

Part your hair on one side, and twist just your bangs. Use bobby pins to secure on the opposite side. This look is great for long, layered bangs.

2.

ADD ACCESSORIES

Barrettes and hair clips can keep growing bangs out of the way without sacrificing style. Headbands and scarves are also great for adding control.

3.

SLICK THEM BACK

Start with damp hair and apply gel to your bangs. Comb your hair back, away from your face. Use hair spray for added hold.

5.

BRAID 'EM

Using hair from your bangs, start French braiding at one side of your forehead, near the roots. Braid across the top of your forehead and angle back, toward your ear. Each time you grab a new section, incorporate a little bit of the rest of your hair. Use bobby pins to secure the ends.

4.

PICK SIDES

A side part can make it easier to style growing bangs. Section bangs when your hair is wet, then blow dry them into a side-swept look.

CHAPTER 8

EVERYDAY ITEMS YOU CAN USE ON YOUR HAIR

The best hair treatments and tools don't always come from a salon. Sometimes they're found in your kitchen.

OLIVE OIL ISN'T JUST FOR COOKING

Fancy salon moisturizing treatments are great, but they can be expensive. You can moisturize any hair length and texture at home with olive oil for a fraction of the cost.

Use the microwave to heat ½ cup of olive oil for 30 seconds. Dip your fingers into the warm oil and massage it into your scalp and down the strands, all the way to the ends. Cover hair with a shower cap and wait 30 minutes. This will give the oil time to work its magic. Rinse your hair with lukewarm water. Then shampoo and rinse again until the oil is completely gone. Condition and style as usual.

MAYO MOISTURIZER

Strands feeling dry? Grab the mayonnaise and transform your hair into a soft and shiny mane. Start with slightly damp hair. Massage ½ cup of full-fat mayonnaise into your scalp and strands, all the way to the ends. If your hair is especially thick or long, you may need a bit more mayo. Use a shower cap to cover your hair for an hour. Rinse hair thoroughly with warm water and then shampoo, condition, and style as usual. You can repeat this treatment weekly to help hydrate very dry tresses.

TUNE OUT THE STATIC

If your hair gets unruly when you take off your hat, static electricity is to blame. Dryer sheets can help keep static electricity from making your hair stand on end. Try these techniques:

✳ Use dryer sheets to wipe down combs and brushes before styling.

✳ Fighting flyaways? Smooth frizz by lightly wiping a dryer sheet over your hair.

✳ Put a dryer sheet inside your pillowcase to keep your hair from building up nighttime static.

BRUSH UP FLY AWAYS

Spray hair spray on the head of an old toothbrush and use it to blend fly-aways in with the rest of your hair. Or, if you have a spare kabuki brush in your makeup bag, use it the same way — it will cover more ground than a toothbrush will.

BOOST FOR BRUNETTES

Do you want to make your dark hair stand out? Give brown or black hair a color boost with coffee. Brew a strong pot, shampoo, and then douse your strands with lukewarm brew. Wrap your head in an old towel and leave the coffee on your head for 10 to 20 minutes before rinsing and adding conditioner.

TREAT DANDRUFF WITH COCONUT OIL

Don't let dandruff flakes get you down. You can battle them with coconut oil. Just follow these simple steps:

WHAT YOU NEED:

3 drops lavender or tea tree oil

2 teaspoons coconut oil

WHAT YOU DO:

Step 1. After washing your hair, mix 2 teaspoons of coconut oil with a few drops of lavender or tea tree oil.

Step 2. Massage the mixture into your scalp and wait 20 to 30 minutes. (You may want to cover your head with a shower cap.)

Step 3. Wash out the oil with a gentle shampoo.

Step 4. Repeat treatment two to three times per week.

LIGHTEN WITH LEMON

Lemon juice is a time-tested way to lighten and add highlights to your hair. This technique works best with heat, so try it on a day you're headed to the beach or pool. Squeeze three large lemons and pour the juice into a spray bottle along with a teaspoon of olive or coconut oil to keep your strands from drying out. Spray the areas of your hair you'd like to lighten. You can go for all over highlights or just the tips. After a few hours in the sun you'll be delighted by the results.

NO DRY SHAMPOO? NO PROBLEM

Dry shampoo can make unwashed hair look fresh again, but what if you don't have any? In a pinch you can use baby powder or cornstarch for the same effect. If you have dark hair, add a little cinnamon or cocoa powder to the mix. Just lightly sprinkle the powder onto your scalp, and comb it through to your roots. Keep combing until you can't see any powder.

EMERGENCY FIXES

Frizz, whether it's caused by static or breakage, can pop up at the worst times. But you can calm those hairs, even if you don't have styling products on hand. All you need is a little lotion. Put a small amount on your palms and carefully rub it over the strands. The hand lotion will weigh down flyaways, creating a smoother look. Make sure you only use a dab. More than that can make your hair look greasy.

DIP-DYE

Colorful tips can be yours with some simple drink mix dip-dyeing.

WHAT YOU NEED:

1 to 3 cups
of water

+

3 to 6 packets of
powdered drink
mix, any color

WHAT TO DO:

Step 1. Start by combing hair and gathering it into a ponytail.

Step 2. Using a medium-sized pan, combine 2 cups of water and three envelopes of powdered drink mix.

Step 3. Stir to dissolve and place on the stove. Bring to a boil and continue to heat the mixture for 2 minutes.

Step 4. Pour the drink mixture into a bowl or cup. Decide how much of your hair you want to color, and then dip that length into the liquid.

Step 5 Leave your hair in the drink mix for 15 to 30 minutes. Light hair generally requires less time, while darker tones require more.

Step 6. When you get the color you want, rinse hair with water.

Step 7. Dry and style as usual. Your color will last longer if you wait a day or two before shampooing. Depending how often you shampoo, the color could last 2 to 4 weeks.

TIP: The darker your hair is, the more drink mix packets you will need.

45

DIY HAIR MASKS

You don't need any special cooking skills to whip up your own hair masks. Raw, natural ingredients are great for creating healthier, silkier hair. And they are often right in your cupboard or refrigerator. DIY your way to shinier locks, and get the healthy hair you've always wanted.

AVOCADO MOISTURIZING MASK
This mask will restore shine while fighting frizz.

WHAT YOU NEED:

1 small, ripe avocado

¼ cup extra-virgin olive oil

1 tablespoon lemon juice

WHAT TO DO:

Step 1. Mash the avocado in a small bowl.

Step 2. Blend the avocado with oil and lemon juice.

Step 3. Apply the mixture to your hair from the ends to the roots. Cover your hair with a plastic shower cap, and let it sit for 15 to 20 minutes.

Step 4. Rinse out the mask. Then wash and condition your hair as usual.

BROWN SUGAR MASK
This mask is great for relieving a dry, itchy scalp.

WHAT YOU NEED:

2 tablespoons brown sugar

1 tablespoon extra-virgin olive oil

WHAT TO DO:

Step 1. Mix the ingredients in a small bowl.

Step 2. Apply the mixture to your hair from top to bottom. Cover your hair with a plastic shower cap, and let it sit for 15 to 20 minutes.

Step 3. Rinse well. Wash and condition as normal.

YOGURT AND HONEY MASK   This protein-rich mask will cleanse, moisturize, and nourish hair.

WHAT YOU NEED:

¼ cup plain yogurt

1 tablespoon honey

1 teaspoon olive oil

 + +

WHAT TO DO:

Step 1. Mix ingredients in a small bowl.

Step 2. Apply the mixture to damp hair. Cover your head with a plastic shower cap, and let it sit for 15 to 20 minutes.

Step 3. Rinse, wash, and condition your hair.

BANANA AND COCONUT OIL MASK   This mask both nourishes and moisturizes hair.

WHAT YOU NEED:

1 very ripe banana

1 tablespoon coconut oil

 +

WHAT TO DO:

Step 1. Using a food processor, blend ingredients until smooth.

Step 2. Apply the mixture to damp hair. Cover your head with a plastic shower cap or warm towel, and let it sit for 20 to 30 minutes.

Step 3. Rinse well. Then wash and condition hair.

READ MORE

Beaumont, M. R. *The Hair Book: Care & Keeping Advice for Girls.* Middleton, Wis.: American Girl Publishing, 2016.

Kenney, Karen Latchana. *Hair Care Tips & Tricks.* New York: Lerner Publications, 2015.

Massey, Lorraine, Michele Bender, and Deborah Chiel. *Curly Girl: The Handbook.* New York: Workman Pub., 2011.

ABOUT THE AUTHOR

Mary Boone has written 34 nonfiction books for young readers on topics ranging from boy bands and fashion designers to crafts and cooking. She also has written for magazines including *Entertainment Weekly* and *People*. Mary and her family live in Tacoma, Washington, where the rain makes her hair forever frizzy.